K. CONNORS

Instagram Branding

Mastering Visual Storytelling and Engagement for Business Success

Copyright © 2024 by K. Connors

All rights reserved. No part of this publication may be reproduced, stored or transmitted in any form or by any means, electronic, mechanical, photocopying, recording, scanning, or otherwise without written permission from the publisher. It is illegal to copy this book, post it to a website, or distribute it by any other means without permission.

First edition

This book was professionally typeset on Reedsy.
Find out more at reedsy.com

Contents

Introduction: The Instagram Advantage	1
Chapter 1: Understanding Instagram as a Platform	5
Chapter 2: Setting Up Your Profile for Success	10
Chapter 3: Developing Your Brand Aesthetic	15
Chapter 4: Content Creation Strategies	20
Chapter 5: Building a Community	25
Chapter 6: Leveraging Hashtags and Trends	30
Chapter 7: Using Instagram Stories Effectively	35
Chapter 8: Analyzing and Optimizing Performance	40
Chapter 9: Monetizing Your Instagram Brand	45
Chapter 10: Staying Ahead of the Curve	50
Conclusion: Wrapping It All Up	55

Introduction: The Instagram Advantage

Welcome to the world of Instagram Branding! Whether you're a seasoned marketer, a budding entrepreneur, or someone who's just curious about the hype, this book is your ultimate guide to mastering the art of building a compelling brand on Instagram. With over a billion active users each month, Instagram isn't just a social media platform; it's a global stage where brands are born, identities are shaped, and dreams come true.

First, let's get one thing straight: Instagram is not just about pretty pictures. Sure, it's where your brunch gets more attention than you do, but it's also where businesses grow, communities form, and ideas spread like wildfire. Instagram has evolved from a simple photo-sharing app to a powerful marketing tool that brands can't afford to ignore.

So why is Instagram so crucial for branding? Let's break it down. In a world where attention spans are shorter than a goldfish's memory, visuals speak louder than words. Instagram's emphasis on visual content makes it the perfect platform to showcase your brand's personality, values, and products. It's where you can tell your story in a way that's engaging, authentic, and yes, aesthetically pleasing.

Instagram's demographic is another key factor in its branding power. The platform is particularly popular among younger audiences, especially Millennials and Gen Z, who are known for their brand loyalty and purchasing power.

If your target audience includes these groups, Instagram is the place to be. But it's not just for the young; Instagram's user base is diverse, with significant representation from different age groups, genders, and locations.

Now, let's talk about the magic of Instagram's algorithm. Understanding how it works can give you a significant edge. The algorithm determines what content gets seen by whom, and it's constantly evolving. While it might seem like a mysterious force, it actually prioritizes content based on engagement, relevance, relationships, and timeliness. This means the more your audience interacts with your content, the more likely it is to be seen by others. Engaging content, therefore, isn't just nice to have; it's essential.

Creating a strong brand on Instagram starts with setting up your profile for success. Your profile is your digital storefront, and first impressions matter. A compelling bio, a recognizable profile picture, and a cohesive aesthetic can make all the difference. Think of your bio as your elevator pitch – it should clearly convey who you are, what you do, and what makes you unique. Your profile picture should be easily identifiable, whether it's your logo or a professional headshot. And your overall aesthetic should reflect your brand's identity, whether that's sleek and modern, vibrant and fun, or anything in between.

Visual consistency is another crucial element of Instagram branding. This doesn't mean every photo needs to look the same, but there should be a cohesive look and feel to your content. This can be achieved through a consistent color palette, filter, or style of photography. Consistency helps in building a recognizable brand identity, which is key to standing out in the crowded Instagram landscape.

Content is king, and on Instagram, this means a variety of posts, stories, reels, and IGTV videos. Each format has its own strengths and can be used strategically to engage your audience. For instance, while regular posts are great for high-quality photos and announcements, stories are perfect

INTRODUCTION: THE INSTAGRAM ADVANTAGE

for behind-the-scenes content, polls, and time-sensitive updates. Reels, Instagram's answer to TikTok, are ideal for short, entertaining videos, while IGTV allows for longer, more in-depth content. Mixing these formats keeps your audience engaged and shows different facets of your brand.

Building a community on Instagram is about more than just gaining followers; it's about creating meaningful interactions. Engaging with your audience by responding to comments, answering DMs, and participating in conversations makes your brand more relatable and trustworthy. Collaborations and partnerships with other brands or influencers can also expand your reach and bring fresh content to your feed. And don't underestimate the power of contests and giveaways – they're not only fun but also a great way to boost engagement and attract new followers.

Hashtags and trends are the secret sauce of Instagram visibility. Hashtags help categorize your content and make it discoverable to a broader audience. Researching and using relevant hashtags can significantly increase your reach. Trends, on the other hand, can provide inspiration for your content and help you stay relevant. However, it's essential to participate in trends that align with your brand's values and voice, rather than jumping on every bandwagon.

Instagram Stories are a game-changer in the realm of social media engagement. With features like polls, questions, stickers, and countdowns, stories are an interactive way to connect with your audience. They offer a sense of urgency, as they disappear after 24 hours, which encourages followers to stay tuned to your updates. Story Highlights can extend the life of your best stories, creating a curated collection of content that new followers can explore.

Analyzing and optimizing your Instagram performance is where the rubber meets the road. Instagram Insights provide valuable data on your audience, content performance, and engagement. Understanding these metrics helps you refine your strategy, improve your content, and ultimately grow your brand. Tools like engagement trackers can also help monitor your progress and identify areas for improvement.

Monetizing your Instagram brand is the dream, isn't it? Sponsored posts, partnerships, and affiliate marketing are popular ways to generate revenue. Attracting sponsors requires a strong, engaged following and high-quality content. Instagram Shopping has made it easier than ever to sell products directly through the app, transforming your feed into a virtual storefront. And affiliate marketing allows you to earn commissions by promoting other brands' products.

Finally, staying ahead of the curve on Instagram is crucial. The platform is always evolving, with new features and trends emerging regularly. Keeping up-to-date with these changes can give you a competitive edge. Experimentation is also vital – don't be afraid to try new things, whether that's a different type of content, a new posting schedule, or a unique collaboration. Continuous learning through courses, books, and other resources can also help you stay on top of your game.

As you can see, Instagram branding is a multifaceted process that requires creativity, strategy, and a deep understanding of the platform. This book will guide you through each step, providing you with the tools and insights you need to build a powerful brand on Instagram. Whether you're starting from scratch or looking to take your existing Instagram presence to the next level, you're in the right place. So, let's dive in and start your journey to Instagram branding success!

Chapter 1: Understanding Instagram as a Platform

Let's start at the beginning. Instagram – the app that's not just an app, but a cultural phenomenon. Since its inception in 2010, Instagram has grown exponentially, transforming the way we interact with the world and each other. What began as a simple photo-sharing platform has evolved into a powerhouse for visual storytelling, marketing, and branding. But how did it get there, and why is it so critical for branding today? Let's dive in.

Instagram's journey is a fascinating one. Launched by Kevin Systrom and Mike Krieger, Instagram was initially an iOS-exclusive app that allowed users to share photos with a variety of filters. Within two months, it had one million users. By April 2012, Facebook saw the potential and acquired Instagram for approximately $1 billion in cash and stock. This acquisition was a game-changer, catapulting Instagram into the big leagues of social media.

The evolution of Instagram has been marked by continuous innovation. From the introduction of video posts in 2013 to the launch of Instagram Stories in 2016, IGTV in 2018, and Reels in 2020, each new feature has kept the platform fresh and engaging. These additions have not only enhanced user experience but also provided brands with more tools to connect with their audience in diverse and dynamic ways.

Now, let's talk numbers. Instagram boasts over one billion monthly active users, with more than 500 million using the platform daily. That's half a billion people scrolling, liking, sharing, and engaging with content every single day. It's not just about quantity, though. The quality of engagement on Instagram is incredibly high, with users spending an average of 30 minutes per day on the app. This presents a golden opportunity for brands to capture and hold their audience's attention.

Understanding Instagram's user demographics is crucial for effective branding. The platform is particularly popular among younger audiences, with 67% of users aged 18-29 and 47% aged 30-49. However, it's not just for the young; 23% of users are aged 50-64, showing that Instagram has broad appeal across age groups. Gender distribution is relatively balanced, with 43% of women and 31% of men using the platform in the United States. Moreover, Instagram has a global reach, with over 80% of users residing outside the U.S., making it a truly international platform.

So, why is Instagram so crucial for branding? The answer lies in its visual nature. Humans are inherently visual creatures – we process images 60,000 times faster than text, and 90% of the information transmitted to our brains is visual. Instagram's emphasis on high-quality images and videos plays to this strength, making it the perfect medium for brands to showcase their products, services, and stories in a visually compelling way.

Moreover, Instagram's algorithm is designed to prioritize engaging content. This means that the more your audience interacts with your posts, the more likely your content is to be seen by others. The algorithm takes into account factors such as the number of likes, comments, shares, and saves a post receives, as well as how quickly these interactions occur. It also considers the relationship between the user and the poster – the more a user engages with a particular account, the more likely they are to see that account's posts in their feed. Understanding these nuances can help brands create content that not only attracts attention but also fosters meaningful engagement.

CHAPTER 1: UNDERSTANDING INSTAGRAM AS A PLATFORM

Setting up your profile for success is the first step in leveraging Instagram's potential. Your profile is essentially your digital storefront – it's the first thing people see when they visit your page, and first impressions matter. A compelling bio is essential; it should succinctly convey who you are, what you do, and what makes you unique. Think of it as your elevator pitch. It's also a good idea to include a call-to-action (CTA) in your bio, such as a link to your website or a specific landing page.

Your profile picture should be easily recognizable. For businesses, this often means using your logo. For personal brands, a professional headshot is usually the way to go. The key is consistency – your profile picture should be the same across all your social media platforms to help with brand recognition.

Visual consistency is another crucial element of a strong Instagram presence. This doesn't mean every photo needs to look the same, but there should be a cohesive look and feel to your content. This can be achieved through a consistent color palette, filter, or style of photography. Consistency helps in building a recognizable brand identity, which is key to standing out in the crowded Instagram landscape.

Instagram's visual-centric platform allows brands to showcase their personality in unique ways. For instance, a fashion brand can use a clean, minimalist aesthetic with neutral tones to convey sophistication and elegance. In contrast, a vibrant, colorful palette can be used to evoke fun and creativity for a children's toy brand. The goal is to ensure that anyone looking at your feed can immediately understand your brand's vibe and values.

Content is the heart of Instagram, and the variety of content formats available allows for creative storytelling. Regular posts are ideal for high-quality images and videos that align with your overall brand aesthetic. Stories, introduced in 2016, offer a more casual and immediate way to engage with your audience. They're perfect for behind-the-scenes content, quick updates, polls, and interactive elements like questions and quizzes. Since stories disappear after

24 hours, they create a sense of urgency and exclusivity.

Reels, Instagram's answer to TikTok, are short, entertaining videos that can be up to 60 seconds long. They're a great way to showcase your brand's fun side and reach new audiences, as Reels have their own dedicated section on the Explore page. IGTV, on the other hand, is designed for longer videos, making it ideal for in-depth content like tutorials, interviews, and product demos.

Building a community on Instagram goes beyond just accumulating followers. It's about creating meaningful interactions and fostering a sense of belonging among your audience. Engaging with your followers by responding to comments, answering DMs, and participating in conversations helps humanize your brand and build trust. Collaborations and partnerships with other brands or influencers can also expand your reach and bring fresh content to your feed. For example, partnering with influencers who align with your brand can introduce your products to their followers, who are likely to trust their recommendations.

Contests and giveaways are another effective way to boost engagement and attract new followers. They're fun, interactive, and provide an incentive for people to follow your account, like your posts, and share your content. A well-executed giveaway can generate a lot of buzz and significantly increase your reach.

Hashtags are a powerful tool for increasing the visibility of your posts. They act as keywords that categorize your content and make it discoverable to a broader audience. Using a mix of popular, niche, and branded hashtags can help you reach different segments of your audience. For instance, while popular hashtags can increase the chances of your post being seen by a large number of users, niche hashtags can help you connect with a more targeted and engaged audience.

Staying relevant and on top of trends is also crucial for Instagram success.

CHAPTER 1: UNDERSTANDING INSTAGRAM AS A PLATFORM

This doesn't mean jumping on every bandwagon, but rather participating in trends that align with your brand's values and voice. Trends can provide inspiration for your content and help you stay relevant in the fast-paced world of social media.

Analyzing and optimizing your performance on Instagram is essential for growth. Instagram Insights offer valuable data on your audience, content performance, and engagement. Understanding these metrics can help you refine your strategy and improve your content. For instance, if you notice that posts with a particular type of content or at a specific time of day perform better, you can adjust your strategy accordingly.

Monetizing your Instagram brand is the dream for many. Sponsored posts, partnerships, and affiliate marketing are popular ways to generate revenue. Attracting sponsors requires a strong, engaged following and high-quality content. Instagram Shopping has made it easier than ever to sell products directly through the app, transforming your feed into a virtual storefront. And affiliate marketing allows you to earn commissions by promoting other brands' products.

Instagram branding is a multifaceted process that requires creativity, strategy, and a deep understanding of the platform. This book will guide you through each step, providing you with the tools and insights you need to build a powerful brand on Instagram. Whether you're starting from scratch or looking to take your existing Instagram presence to the next level, you're in the right place. So, let's dive in and start your journey to Instagram branding success!

Chapter 2: Setting Up Your Profile for Success

Alright, so you're ready to make waves on Instagram. But before you start posting those stunning photos and engaging videos, you need to nail the basics: setting up your profile for success. Think of your profile as your digital storefront. It's the first thing people see when they visit your page, and first impressions matter. Let's break down the key elements that will help you create a profile that stands out from the crowd.

First up, your Instagram bio. This little snippet of text might seem trivial, but it's actually one of the most important parts of your profile. Your bio is your elevator pitch – it should clearly convey who you are, what you do, and what makes you unique, all in 150 characters or less. It's a tall order, but with a little creativity, you can craft a bio that's both informative and engaging.

Start with the basics: who you are and what you do. If you're a business, make sure your brand name is front and center. If you're a personal brand, use your real name or a memorable handle that reflects your identity. Next, highlight what you offer. Are you a fitness coach? A fashion blogger? A tech startup? Be specific about what you bring to the table.

A touch of personality can go a long way in making your bio memorable. Whether it's a witty tagline, a clever emoji, or a branded hashtag, these little details can help you stand out and give followers a glimpse of your brand's character. For example, a travel blogger might use a globe emoji and a tagline like "Wandering the world, one adventure at a time." A fitness coach might use a flexing bicep emoji and a slogan like "Helping you get fit, one rep at a time."

Don't forget to include a call-to-action (CTA) in your bio. This could be a link to your website, a specific landing page, or a recent blog post. Instagram allows you to add one clickable link in your bio, so make it count. If you have multiple links you want to share, consider using a service like Linktree, which allows you to create a custom landing page with multiple links.

Next, let's talk about your profile picture. Your profile picture should be easily recognizable and consistent with your branding across other social media platforms. For businesses, this often means using your logo. For personal brands, a professional headshot is usually the way to go. The key is to make sure your profile picture is high-quality and easily identifiable, even when it's displayed as a small thumbnail.

Now, onto your username and handle. Your username is your identity on Instagram, so choose wisely. Ideally, it should be the same or very similar to your handle on other social media platforms to ensure consistency. Avoid using numbers or special characters unless absolutely necessary, as they can make your handle harder to remember.

Visual consistency is another crucial element of a strong Instagram profile. This doesn't mean every photo needs to look the same, but there should be a cohesive look and feel to your content. This can be achieved through a consistent color palette, filter, or style of photography. For example, if you use a particular filter on your photos, use it consistently to create a uniform look across your feed. This helps in building a recognizable brand identity, which is key to standing out in the crowded Instagram landscape.

Highlights are a fantastic way to keep your best content front and center. They appear just below your bio and above your feed, providing a great way to showcase important information, evergreen content, or themed collections. Think of them as curated albums that give new visitors a quick overview of what your brand is all about. For example, a restaurant might have highlights for their menu, customer reviews, and behind-the-scenes content. A fashion brand might create highlights for new arrivals, sales, and user-generated content.

Setting up your account settings properly is another essential step. Switching to a business or creator account can unlock additional features that can help you grow your brand. These accounts provide access to Instagram Insights, which offer valuable data on your audience, content performance, and engagement. Business accounts also allow you to add contact buttons to your profile, making it easier for followers to get in touch with you.

Privacy settings are also important to consider. While it's generally a good idea to keep your account public if you're trying to build a brand, you should still review your settings to make sure you're comfortable with how your data is being used and shared. Instagram allows you to control who can comment on your posts, who can tag you, and who can message you, among other things. Take the time to review these settings and adjust them to suit your needs.

Now that we've covered the basics, let's talk about optimizing your content strategy. Posting high-quality content consistently is key to growing your Instagram presence. But what does "high-quality" mean? It's about more than just pretty pictures. Your content should be visually appealing, yes, but it should also be relevant to your audience and aligned with your brand's voice and values.

Planning your content in advance can help ensure that you're posting consistently and strategically. A content calendar can be a valuable tool for this. It allows you to map out what you're going to post and when, so you can maintain a consistent presence without feeling overwhelmed. When planning your content, consider a mix of different types of posts, such as photos, videos, carousels, and stories, to keep your feed interesting and engaging.

Engaging captions are another important aspect of your content strategy. A good caption can add context to your photos, showcase your brand's personality, and encourage interaction from your followers. When writing captions, consider using a mix of storytelling, humor, and calls-to-action to engage your audience. For example, you could share a behind-the-scenes story about how a product was made, use a funny anecdote to entertain your followers, or ask a question to encourage comments.

Hashtags are a powerful tool for increasing the visibility of your posts. They act as keywords that categorize your content and make it discoverable to a broader audience. Researching and using relevant hashtags can significantly increase your reach. A good strategy is to use a mix of popular, niche, and branded hashtags. Popular hashtags can increase the chances of your post being seen by a large number of users, while niche hashtags can help you connect with a more targeted and engaged audience. Branded hashtags, which are unique to your brand, can help you build a community around your content.

Engagement is the lifeblood of Instagram. It's not just about the number of followers you have, but how engaged they are with your content. Responding to comments and direct messages promptly and authentically can help build a loyal community of followers who feel valued and connected to your brand. Engaging with other users' content by liking, commenting, and sharing can also increase your visibility and foster relationships within your niche.

Collaborations and partnerships can be a powerful way to expand your reach and bring fresh content to your feed. Partnering with influencers who align with your brand can introduce your products to their followers, who are likely to trust their recommendations. Collaborations can take many forms, from co-hosting Instagram Lives to creating joint content or running giveaways.

Finally, let's talk about the importance of analyzing your performance and optimizing your strategy. Instagram Insights provide valuable data on your audience, content performance, and engagement. Understanding these metrics can help you refine your strategy and improve your content. For example, if you notice that posts with a particular type of content or at a specific time of day perform better, you can adjust your strategy accordingly. Regularly reviewing your performance and making data-driven decisions is key to growing your Instagram presence and achieving your branding goals.

Setting up your profile for success on Instagram is about more than just filling out the basic information. It's about creating a cohesive, engaging, and visually appealing presence that reflects your brand's identity and values. By paying attention to the details and being strategic about your content and engagement, you can create a profile that not only attracts followers but also builds a loyal and engaged community.

Chapter 3: Developing Your Brand Aesthetic

Now that you've got your profile set up and ready to go, it's time to dive into one of the most crucial aspects of Instagram branding: developing your brand aesthetic. A strong and cohesive visual identity is what sets successful brands apart from the rest. It's what makes someone stop scrolling and take notice of your content. So, let's unpack how you can create a visually stunning Instagram presence that truly represents your brand.

First things first, let's talk about visual consistency. Consistency doesn't mean every photo needs to look identical, but your overall feed should have a cohesive look and feel. This can be achieved through a consistent color palette, filter, or style of photography. Think of your Instagram feed as a digital magazine – it should have a unified theme that reflects your brand's personality and values.

Choosing a color palette is a great starting point. Colors evoke emotions and can significantly impact how your brand is perceived. For example, blue is often associated with trust and calmness, while red can evoke excitement and urgency. Think about the emotions you want to convey and select a palette that aligns with those feelings. Stick to two or three primary colors and use them consistently across your posts. This doesn't mean every photo has to be dominated by these colors, but they should be present in some way, whether it's through backgrounds, props, or even the lighting.

Filters and editing styles also play a big role in creating a cohesive aesthetic. Whether you prefer bright and airy, dark and moody, or vibrant and colorful, choose a filter that complements your brand's identity and use it consistently. Many successful Instagram brands use a signature filter or preset to maintain a uniform look across their feed. There are plenty of apps and tools available, like Adobe Lightroom, VSCO, and Snapseed, that can help you achieve the desired look.

Photography style is another critical component of your brand aesthetic. Consider the composition, lighting, and subject matter of your photos. Are you going for a minimalist look with lots of negative space, or do you prefer a more detailed and busy composition? Do you want your photos to have a natural, candid feel, or are you aiming for a more polished and professional look? Whatever your style, consistency is key. Your audience should be able to recognize your photos even without seeing your handle.

Let's move on to the types of content that will populate your visually stunning feed. Variety is essential, but it's also important to maintain a balance and ensure everything aligns with your brand's overall aesthetic. High-quality images of your products or services should be a staple. Showcase them in different settings and contexts to highlight their features and benefits. Use close-ups to show details and wider shots to provide context.

User-generated content (UGC) is another fantastic way to add variety to your feed while also building community and credibility. Encourage your customers to share photos of themselves using your products and repost these on your feed. UGC not only provides authentic content but also helps potential customers see real-life examples of how your products are used and loved.

Behind-the-scenes content adds a personal touch and helps humanize your brand. Share photos and videos of your team at work, your creative process, or how your products are made. This type of content gives your audience a glimpse into the inner workings of your brand and helps build a deeper connection.

Quotes and text-based posts can also be a valuable addition to your feed, especially if they align with your brand's message and values. Use your brand's fonts and colors to create visually appealing graphics. These types of posts can break up the visual monotony and provide inspirational or educational content to your audience.

Now that we've covered the visual elements, let's talk about planning and curating your feed. A content calendar is an invaluable tool for maintaining consistency and organization. Plan your posts at least a month in advance, considering any upcoming events, product launches, or campaigns. This ensures that you're always prepared and can maintain a steady flow of content.

There are several tools available that can help you plan and preview your Instagram feed, such as Planoly, Later, and Preview. These tools allow you to see how your posts will look together, ensuring a cohesive and visually appealing feed. They also offer scheduling features, so you can plan and automate your posts in advance, saving you time and ensuring consistency.

Another important aspect of your brand aesthetic is your use of Instagram Stories. While your main feed should have a cohesive look, Stories offer a bit more flexibility and can be used for more spontaneous and varied content. However, maintaining some level of consistency is still important. Use your brand's colors and fonts in your Stories, and consider creating templates for different types of content, such as announcements, behind-the-scenes glimpses, or user-generated content.

Highlights are a fantastic way to extend the life of your Stories and keep important content easily accessible. Organize your highlights into categories that make sense for your brand, such as "New Arrivals," "Behind the Scenes,"

"Customer Reviews," or "Tips and Tricks." Create custom highlight covers that match your brand's aesthetic to keep everything looking polished and professional.

Consistency in your visual identity extends beyond just your Instagram feed. It should be reflected in all your digital and physical touchpoints, from your website and email marketing to your packaging and in-store displays. This creates a cohesive brand experience for your audience, reinforcing your brand identity and making it more memorable.

Let's talk about some practical tips for creating high-quality visual content. First, invest in a good camera or smartphone with a high-quality camera. While it's possible to create great content with just a smartphone, having a good camera can significantly improve the quality of your photos and videos.

Lighting is crucial for creating professional-looking photos. Natural light is often the best, so try to shoot your photos near windows or outside during the golden hours – just after sunrise and before sunset – when the light is soft and flattering. If natural light isn't an option, invest in some good artificial lighting, such as a ring light or softbox.

Composition is another important factor. Use the rule of thirds to create balanced and visually appealing photos. This involves dividing your frame into a grid of nine equal parts and placing your subject along these lines or at their intersections. Experiment with different angles and perspectives to add variety and interest to your photos.

Editing is where you can really bring your brand's aesthetic to life. Consistent editing helps to maintain a cohesive look across your feed. Start with basic adjustments like brightness, contrast, and saturation, and then apply your chosen filter or preset. Don't overdo it – the goal is to enhance your photos, not to make them look overly edited or unnatural.

CHAPTER 3: DEVELOPING YOUR BRAND AESTHETIC

Incorporating video content into your strategy is another great way to enhance your brand aesthetic. Videos can showcase your products in action, provide tutorials or demonstrations, and share behind-the-scenes glimpses of your brand. Keep your videos short and engaging, and make sure they align with your overall visual style.

Instagram Reels are a fantastic way to add a dynamic element to your feed. These short, entertaining videos can be a great way to showcase your brand's personality and creativity. Use Reels to share quick tips, product highlights, or fun behind-the-scenes moments. Since Reels have their own dedicated section on the Explore page, they can also help you reach new audiences and increase your visibility.

Finally, don't forget the importance of engagement. A beautiful feed will attract followers, but engagement is what will keep them around. Respond to comments, like and comment on other users' posts, and use Instagram's interactive features like polls, questions, and quizzes in your Stories. This not only boosts your engagement metrics but also helps build a loyal and engaged community around your brand.

Developing a strong brand aesthetic on Instagram is about more than just creating pretty pictures. It's about crafting a visual identity that reflects your brand's personality, values, and message. By paying attention to the details and being consistent in your visual style, you can create a compelling and memorable Instagram presence that stands out from the crowd.

Chapter 4: Content Creation Strategies

So, you've got your profile set up and your brand aesthetic nailed down. Now comes the fun part: content creation. Creating engaging, high-quality content is the backbone of a successful Instagram presence. It's not just about pretty pictures and catchy captions; it's about telling your brand's story in a way that resonates with your audience. Let's dive into the nitty-gritty of crafting a content strategy that works.

First, let's talk about the different types of content you can create on Instagram. The platform offers a variety of formats, each with its own strengths and opportunities for engagement. Understanding these formats and how to use them effectively is key to a well-rounded content strategy.

Regular posts are the bread and butter of Instagram content. These can be photos, videos, or carousels (multiple images or videos in a single post). Photos should be high-quality and visually appealing, reflecting your brand's aesthetic. Videos can be up to 60 seconds long and are perfect for showcasing products in action, sharing behind-the-scenes glimpses, or telling a story that's better conveyed through motion.

Carousels are particularly useful for sharing multiple angles of a product, step-by-step tutorials, or a series of related images. They encourage users to swipe through and spend more time on your post, which can boost your engagement metrics.

CHAPTER 4: CONTENT CREATION STRATEGIES

Instagram Stories, introduced in 2016, are a game-changer. They allow you to share photos and videos that disappear after 24 hours, creating a sense of urgency and exclusivity. Stories are perfect for more spontaneous, behind-the-scenes content, time-sensitive announcements, and interactive features like polls, questions, and quizzes. The ephemeral nature of Stories encourages followers to check back frequently to see what's new, keeping your brand top-of-mind.

Reels, Instagram's answer to TikTok, are short, engaging videos that can be up to 60 seconds long. They're great for showcasing your brand's personality and creativity in a fun, entertaining format. Reels have their own dedicated section on the Explore page, making them a powerful tool for reaching new audiences and increasing your visibility.

IGTV, or Instagram TV, is designed for longer videos, up to 60 minutes for verified accounts and 10 minutes for others. IGTV is ideal for in-depth content like tutorials, interviews, and product demos. It allows you to dive deeper into topics and provide valuable information to your audience.

Live videos are another powerful tool for real-time engagement. Going live allows you to interact with your audience in real-time, answer their questions, and build a sense of community. Live videos can be used for Q&A sessions, product launches, or virtual events. They're a great way to foster a deeper connection with your audience and make your brand more approachable.

Now that we've covered the different content formats, let's talk about planning your content. A well-thought-out content calendar is essential for maintaining consistency and organization. Start by mapping out key dates and events relevant to your brand, such as product launches, holidays, or industry events. This helps ensure that your content is timely and relevant.

Next, brainstorm content ideas for each of these key dates and events. Consider a mix of different types of posts to keep your feed interesting and engaging.

For example, you might plan a carousel post to showcase a new product, a series of Stories to give a behind-the-scenes look at the production process, and a Reel to highlight customer testimonials.

Once you have a list of content ideas, organize them into a calendar. This can be a simple spreadsheet or a more sophisticated tool like Planoly, Later, or Trello. Scheduling your posts in advance not only helps you stay organized but also ensures that you're posting consistently. Consistency is key to keeping your audience engaged and building a loyal following.

Creating engaging captions is another important aspect of your content strategy. Captions add context to your photos and videos, showcase your brand's personality, and encourage interaction from your followers. A good caption should be informative, engaging, and aligned with your brand's voice.

When writing captions, consider using a mix of storytelling, humor, and calls-to-action. Storytelling helps to create an emotional connection with your audience, making your content more relatable and memorable. Humor adds a lighthearted touch and can make your brand more approachable. Calls-to-action encourage your followers to engage with your content by liking, commenting, or sharing.

For example, if you're sharing a photo of a new product, you might write a caption that tells the story behind its creation, adds a humorous anecdote about the development process, and ends with a call-to-action like "Tell us your thoughts in the comments!" or "Tap the link in our bio to learn more!"

Hashtags are another powerful tool for increasing the visibility of your posts. They act as keywords that categorize your content and make it discoverable to a broader audience. Using a mix of popular, niche, and branded hashtags can help you reach different segments of your audience.

Popular hashtags can increase the chances of your post being seen by a large

CHAPTER 4: CONTENT CREATION STRATEGIES

number of users, but they're also highly competitive. Niche hashtags, on the other hand, have a smaller, more targeted audience, which can lead to higher engagement rates. Branded hashtags, which are unique to your brand, can help you build a community around your content and encourage user-generated content.

When choosing hashtags, research and use ones that are relevant to your content and audience. Tools like Hashtagify, All Hashtag, and Instagram's own search feature can help you find the best hashtags for your posts. Aim for a mix of broad and specific hashtags to maximize your reach and engagement.

Engagement is the lifeblood of Instagram. It's not just about the number of followers you have, but how engaged they are with your content. Responding to comments and direct messages promptly and authentically can help build a loyal community of followers who feel valued and connected to your brand. Engaging with other users' content by liking, commenting, and sharing can also increase your visibility and foster relationships within your niche.

Collaborations and partnerships are another effective way to expand your reach and bring fresh content to your feed. Partnering with influencers who align with your brand can introduce your products to their followers, who are likely to trust their recommendations. Collaborations can take many forms, from co-hosting Instagram Lives to creating joint content or running giveaways.

Analyzing and optimizing your performance is essential for growth. Instagram Insights provide valuable data on your audience, content performance, and engagement. Understanding these metrics can help you refine your strategy and improve your content.

Key metrics to track include reach, impressions, engagement rate, and follower growth. Reach is the number of unique users who see your content, while impressions are the total number of times your content is viewed.

Engagement rate is the percentage of your followers who interact with your content, and follower growth tracks how your audience is growing over time.

Regularly reviewing your performance and making data-driven decisions is key to growing your Instagram presence and achieving your branding goals. For example, if you notice that posts with a particular type of content or at a specific time of day perform better, you can adjust your strategy accordingly.

Creating high-quality content consistently is the backbone of a successful Instagram presence. By understanding the different content formats, planning your content in advance, writing engaging captions, using hashtags effectively, and analyzing your performance, you can create a content strategy that resonates with your audience and helps you achieve your branding goals.

Remember, it's not just about pretty pictures and catchy captions; it's about telling your brand's story in a way that resonates with your audience. With a well-thought-out content strategy, you can build a strong and engaged community on Instagram that's excited to follow your brand's journey.

Chapter 5: Building a Community

Alright, you've got your profile looking sharp, your brand aesthetic on point, and a killer content strategy in place. Now it's time to focus on one of the most crucial aspects of Instagram branding: building a community. A loyal and engaged community is the foundation of any successful brand on Instagram. It's what turns casual followers into dedicated fans and customers. Let's dive into the strategies and tactics for fostering a vibrant and interactive community around your brand.

Engagement is the lifeblood of a thriving Instagram community. It's not just about the number of followers you have, but how actively they interact with your content. Responding to comments and direct messages promptly and authentically can help build a loyal following. When someone takes the time to comment on your post or send you a message, it's an opportunity to engage in a meaningful conversation. This personal touch can make followers feel valued and more connected to your brand.

Think about the tone and style of your responses. If your brand has a casual and friendly vibe, keep your replies light-hearted and fun. If your brand is more formal, maintain a professional tone while still being personable. The key is to be consistent with your brand voice and make each interaction feel genuine.

Creating interactive content is another effective way to boost engagement.

Instagram Stories are perfect for this. Use features like polls, questions, and quizzes to encourage followers to interact with your content. Polls can be a great way to get feedback on new product ideas or simply to entertain your audience. Questions allow followers to engage more deeply by sharing their thoughts or asking you about your brand. Quizzes can be a fun way to educate your audience about your products or industry.

User-generated content (UGC) is a goldmine for building community. Encouraging your followers to create and share content related to your brand not only provides you with authentic, high-quality content but also makes your followers feel like they are part of your brand's story. You can do this by creating a branded hashtag and encouraging your followers to use it when they post about your products or services. Repost the best UGC on your feed and Stories, giving credit to the original creators. This not only acknowledges your followers' contributions but also encourages more people to join in.

Contests and giveaways are another powerful tool for building community. They're not only fun and engaging but also a great way to attract new followers and boost engagement. When planning a contest, make sure the prize is something that will genuinely excite your audience. It doesn't have to be expensive, but it should be relevant to your brand and valuable to your followers. Set clear and simple rules for participation, such as liking the post, following your account, tagging friends, or sharing a photo with your branded hashtag. This not only increases engagement but also helps spread the word about your brand.

Collaborations and partnerships can also play a significant role in community building. Partnering with influencers or other brands that align with your values and target audience can help you reach new followers and add credibility to your brand. When choosing collaborators, look for those who have an engaged and loyal following, rather than just a large number of followers. A well-planned collaboration can introduce your brand to a whole new audience and create exciting content that resonates with both your followers and those of your collaborator.

Hosting Instagram Live sessions is a fantastic way to engage with your community in real-time. Live videos allow you to interact directly with your audience, answer their questions, and build a deeper connection. You can use Live sessions for Q&A sessions, product launches, behind-the-scenes tours, or interviews with industry experts. The real-time nature of Live videos creates a sense of immediacy and exclusivity, encouraging more followers to tune in and engage.

Creating a sense of exclusivity can also help build a strong community. Offering exclusive content or early access to new products for your Instagram followers can make them feel special and valued. This could be in the form of sneak peeks, limited-time discounts, or special events. The idea is to give your followers a reason to stay engaged and keep coming back for more.

Understanding and leveraging Instagram Insights is crucial for community building. Insights provide valuable data on your audience's demographics, behaviors, and engagement patterns. This information can help you tailor your content and engagement strategies to better meet the needs and preferences of your followers. For example, if you notice that a significant portion of your audience is located in a particular time zone, you can schedule your posts to go live when they are most active. If you see that certain types of content consistently receive higher engagement, you can create more of that content.

Creating a community on Instagram is not just about your own efforts but also about fostering interactions among your followers. Encouraging followers to engage with each other can create a sense of belonging and camaraderie. You can do this by asking questions in your captions, prompting discussions, or hosting community events like virtual meetups or challenges. When followers interact with each other, it strengthens the overall community and deepens their connection to your brand.

Maintaining authenticity is key to building a genuine and loyal community. In a world where consumers are increasingly savvy and skeptical, authenticity can set your brand apart. Be transparent about your brand's values, mission, and behind-the-scenes processes. Share your successes and challenges, and be honest in your interactions. Authenticity builds trust, and trust is the foundation of a strong community.

Listening to your audience is just as important as engaging with them. Pay attention to the feedback and suggestions you receive from your followers. Whether it's through comments, direct messages, or polls, listening to your audience can provide valuable insights into their needs and preferences. Use this feedback to improve your products, services, and content strategy. When followers see that you value their input and take their suggestions seriously, they are more likely to feel connected to your brand and remain loyal.

Storytelling is a powerful tool for community building. Sharing the story behind your brand, your products, and your team can create an emotional connection with your audience. Use your captions, Stories, and IGTV videos to tell these stories in an engaging and relatable way. Highlight customer stories and testimonials to show the real-life impact of your products. When followers see themselves reflected in your brand's story, it deepens their connection and fosters a sense of community.

Investing in customer service on Instagram is also essential for community building. Responding to customer inquiries and addressing concerns promptly and professionally can enhance your brand's reputation and build trust. Use direct messages to provide personalized support and resolve issues. A positive customer service experience can turn a follower into a loyal advocate for your brand.

Building a community on Instagram is a multifaceted process that requires ongoing effort and dedication. By focusing on engagement, creating interactive content, leveraging user-generated content, hosting contests and giveaways, collaborating with influencers, and maintaining authenticity, you can foster a vibrant and loyal community around your brand. A strong community not only enhances your brand's presence on Instagram but also drives long-term success and growth.

Chapter 6: Leveraging Hashtags and Trends

Let's talk about hashtags and trends – the secret weapons of Instagram success. These little tools pack a powerful punch when it comes to boosting visibility and engagement on your posts. But like any tool, their effectiveness depends on how well you use them. Let's break down the strategies for leveraging hashtags and trends to elevate your Instagram game.

Hashtags are essentially the keywords of Instagram. They categorize your content and make it discoverable to a broader audience. When users search for a particular hashtag or click on one in a post, they're taken to a feed of all posts that include that hashtag. This can significantly increase the reach of your content beyond your immediate followers.

Choosing the right hashtags is crucial. Start with research. Look at the hashtags that similar brands and influencers in your niche are using. Instagram's search function is a helpful tool for this. Simply type in a keyword related to your content, and Instagram will suggest related hashtags along with their usage count. Aim for a mix of popular, moderately popular, and niche hashtags.

Popular hashtags have millions of posts associated with them. While they can potentially reach a large audience, they're also highly competitive, meaning your content can easily get lost in the sea of posts. Moderately popular hashtags, which have fewer posts, can strike a balance by reaching a good

CHAPTER 6: LEVERAGING HASHTAGS AND TRENDS

number of users while still allowing your content to stand out. Niche hashtags, on the other hand, are more specific and have a smaller, more targeted audience. These can lead to higher engagement rates as the users searching these hashtags are often more interested in the specific content you're posting.

Branded hashtags are unique to your brand and can be an effective way to build community and encourage user-generated content. Create a branded hashtag that's easy to remember and reflects your brand's identity. Encourage your followers to use this hashtag when they post about your products or services. This not only increases the visibility of your brand but also helps you easily find and engage with user-generated content.

Using location-based hashtags can also boost the reach of your posts, especially if your business has a physical presence or serves a specific geographical area. Adding location-specific hashtags can attract local users who might be interested in visiting your store or using your services.

Let's move on to the art of trendspotting. Trends are a big part of what makes Instagram tick. Jumping on relevant trends can give your content a significant visibility boost. But, it's important to approach trends strategically. Not every trend will align with your brand, and chasing trends just for the sake of it can come off as inauthentic.

Start by identifying trends that align with your brand's values and message. Follow industry leaders, influencers, and competitors to see what trends they're participating in. Keep an eye on the Explore page and popular hashtags to spot emerging trends. Tools like Google Trends and social media listening tools can also help you track trending topics and hashtags.

When participating in a trend, put your own unique spin on it. This helps your content stand out while still being part of the broader conversation. For example, if there's a trending challenge or meme, think about how you can adapt it to fit your brand's voice and aesthetic. This not only makes your content relevant but also reinforces your brand identity.

Another effective way to leverage trends is through seasonal and event-based content. Holidays, cultural events, and industry-specific events provide excellent opportunities to create timely and relevant content. Plan your content calendar around these events and use relevant hashtags to increase the visibility of your posts. For example, if you're a fitness brand, creating content around New Year's resolutions or summer fitness goals can attract a lot of engagement.

Instagram Stories are a great way to participate in trends and keep your content fresh. The ephemeral nature of Stories makes them perfect for timely and trend-based content. Use features like polls, questions, and countdowns to engage with your audience around trending topics. Reposting relevant user-generated content in your Stories can also help you tap into trends while building community.

Reels are another powerful tool for trend-based content. Their short, engaging format makes them ideal for participating in trending challenges, dances, or memes. Since Reels have their own dedicated section on the Explore page, they can significantly increase your visibility and attract new followers. Keep an eye on trending sounds and effects, and think about how you can incorporate them into your Reels in a way that aligns with your brand.

Analyzing the performance of your hashtags and trend-based content is essential for refining your strategy. Instagram Insights provide valuable data on the reach and engagement of your posts, including the performance of individual hashtags. Use this data to identify which hashtags and trends are driving the most engagement and adjust your strategy accordingly.

Consistency is key when it comes to using hashtags. Develop a set of core hashtags that you use regularly, along with a rotating selection of additional hashtags that are relevant to specific posts. This not only helps in maintaining a cohesive brand presence but also increases the chances of your content being discovered by new users.

Creating a hashtag strategy involves more than just slapping a bunch of hashtags onto your posts. It's about understanding the nuances of each hashtag and how it fits into your overall content strategy. Pay attention to the context and relevance of each hashtag. Using too many unrelated hashtags can make your posts look spammy and reduce engagement. Aim for a mix of 10 to 30 relevant hashtags per post, depending on the platform's limits and your specific goals.

Engaging with the content in the hashtags you use is another effective strategy. Don't just use hashtags passively; actively participate in the conversations happening around them. Like, comment, and share posts from other users in your hashtag communities. This not only increases your visibility but also helps build relationships within your niche.

Incorporating trending topics into your content doesn't mean you have to abandon your core content themes. Instead, think about how you can weave trends into your existing content strategy. This ensures that your content remains authentic and aligned with your brand, while still being relevant and timely.

Let's not forget about the importance of monitoring the effectiveness of your hashtag and trend strategies. Regularly review your Instagram Insights to track the performance of your posts and hashtags. Look at metrics like reach, impressions, engagement rate, and follower growth to understand what's working and what's not. Use this data to refine your approach and continuously improve your strategy.

Remember, the goal of using hashtags and trends is not just to increase visibility but to engage with your audience in meaningful ways. Focus on creating high-quality content that resonates with your followers and reflects your brand's identity. When used effectively, hashtags and trends can be powerful tools for growing your Instagram presence and building a loyal, engaged community.

Chapter 7: Using Instagram Stories Effectively

Instagram Stories have transformed the way users interact with content on the platform. Introduced in 2016, Stories allow users to share photos and videos that disappear after 24 hours, creating a sense of urgency and exclusivity. They offer a versatile and dynamic way to engage with your audience, and when used effectively, they can significantly boost your brand's visibility and engagement. Let's delve into the strategies for using Instagram Stories to their fullest potential.

First, understand the unique nature of Stories. Unlike regular posts that remain on your profile, Stories are temporary. This ephemerality encourages followers to check your updates frequently, ensuring that your content is always fresh and relevant. Stories also appear at the top of the Instagram feed, making them highly visible and easy to access.

Visual appeal is crucial for Instagram Stories. Given their fleeting nature, your Stories need to capture attention quickly. Use high-quality images and videos that are visually striking. Bright colors, bold text, and compelling visuals can help your Stories stand out. Don't be afraid to experiment with different formats and styles to see what resonates best with your audience.

Instagram offers a variety of tools and features to enhance your Stories.

Stickers are one of the most versatile tools available. You can use location stickers to tag specific places, which can help local users discover your content. Hashtag stickers make your Stories searchable, increasing their visibility. Mention stickers allow you to tag other users, which can encourage them to share your Story with their followers, amplifying your reach.

Interactive stickers are particularly effective for boosting engagement. Polls, questions, and quizzes invite your audience to participate in your content actively. For example, you can use polls to gather feedback on new products or services, ask questions to understand your audience's preferences better, or create quizzes related to your brand or industry. These interactive elements make your Stories more engaging and provide valuable insights into your audience's interests and behaviors.

The countdown sticker is another powerful tool for creating excitement around upcoming events, product launches, or sales. By setting a countdown, you can build anticipation and remind your followers about important dates. This can drive engagement and encourage followers to return to your profile to check for updates.

Story Highlights extend the life of your best Stories, making them accessible even after the 24-hour window has passed. Highlights appear just below your bio on your profile, providing a great way to showcase evergreen content, important information, or themed collections. Organize your Highlights into categories that make sense for your brand, such as "New Arrivals," "Behind the Scenes," "Customer Reviews," or "Tips and Tricks." Create custom covers for your Highlights to keep everything looking cohesive and professional.

Consistency is key to maintaining a strong presence with Instagram Stories. Posting regularly keeps your audience engaged and coming back for more. Develop a content calendar specifically for Stories, planning out what you'll share each day. This ensures that you always have fresh content ready to go and helps you maintain a consistent posting schedule.

CHAPTER 7: USING INSTAGRAM STORIES EFFECTIVELY

Behind-the-scenes content is perfect for Stories. It gives your audience a glimpse into the inner workings of your brand, humanizing your business and building a deeper connection. Share photos and videos of your team at work, your creative process, or how your products are made. This type of content adds a personal touch and makes your brand more relatable.

User-generated content (UGC) is another fantastic option for Stories. Encourage your followers to share photos and videos of themselves using your products and tag you in their posts. Repost the best UGC in your Stories, giving credit to the original creators. This not only provides authentic content but also makes your followers feel appreciated and involved in your brand's community.

Educational content can also be highly effective in Stories. Share tips, tutorials, or how-to guides related to your products or industry. Break down complex information into easily digestible segments, using a series of photos or short videos. Use text overlays to highlight key points and ensure your message is clear, even if viewers are watching without sound.

Promotional content should be a part of your Stories strategy, but it's essential to strike a balance. Constantly pushing sales messages can turn off your audience. Instead, mix promotional content with engaging, entertaining, and informative posts. When you do promote your products or services, make sure to add value, such as exclusive discounts, special offers, or early access for your Instagram followers.

Analytics are crucial for optimizing your Stories strategy. Instagram Insights provide valuable data on how your Stories are performing, including metrics like reach, impressions, taps forward, taps back, and exits. Use this data to understand what type of content resonates most with your audience and adjust your strategy accordingly. For example, if you notice that certain types of Stories consistently receive higher engagement, create more of that content.

Collaborations and takeovers can add a fresh perspective to your Stories and introduce your brand to new audiences. Partner with influencers, industry experts, or complementary brands to create joint content. A takeover, where a guest takes over your Stories for a day, can be particularly engaging. It provides unique content for your followers and leverages the guest's audience, potentially attracting new followers to your profile.

Cross-promotion is another effective tactic. Promote your Stories on other platforms, such as your website, email newsletters, or other social media channels. This can drive traffic to your Instagram profile and increase the visibility of your Stories. Similarly, use your Stories to promote other content, such as new posts, blog articles, or YouTube videos.

Live videos are a powerful extension of Stories. Going live allows you to interact with your audience in real-time, answer their questions, and build a deeper connection. Use Live sessions for Q&A sessions, product launches, behind-the-scenes tours, or interviews with industry experts. The real-time nature of Live videos creates a sense of immediacy and exclusivity, encouraging more followers to tune in and engage.

Highlighting customer stories and testimonials in your Stories can build trust and credibility. Share photos and videos of satisfied customers using your products, along with their reviews or testimonials. This not only showcases the value of your products but also provides social proof, which can be highly persuasive.

Creating a series of Stories around a specific theme or campaign can help maintain consistency and keep your audience engaged. For example, you might create a weekly series where you share industry news, highlight a product of the week, or provide tips and advice related to your niche. Consistent series give your followers something to look forward to and can help establish a routine of engagement.

CHAPTER 7: USING INSTAGRAM STORIES EFFECTIVELY

Don't overlook the power of storytelling in your Stories. Use the narrative format to tell compelling stories that resonate with your audience. Whether it's the story behind a product, a customer success story, or a day in the life of your team, storytelling can create an emotional connection and make your content more memorable.

Engaging with your audience is crucial for building a loyal community. Respond to messages and comments on your Stories, and show appreciation for your followers' feedback and contributions. This two-way interaction fosters a sense of connection and loyalty, encouraging followers to engage with your content regularly.

Finally, stay creative and experiment with new ideas and formats. The dynamic nature of Stories means there's always room to try something new and see what works best for your audience. Keep an eye on trends and be willing to adapt your strategy as needed. By staying flexible and creative, you can continue to keep your content fresh, engaging, and relevant.

Using Instagram Stories effectively requires a combination of creativity, consistency, and strategic planning. By leveraging the various tools and features available, maintaining a regular posting schedule, and continuously analyzing your performance, you can create Stories that captivate your audience and strengthen your brand's presence on Instagram.

Chapter 8: Analyzing and Optimizing Performance

So, you've been posting away on Instagram, engaging with your followers, and creating killer content. But how do you know if all your efforts are actually paying off? That's where analyzing and optimizing your performance comes into play. Understanding your Instagram metrics and making data-driven decisions are crucial steps in refining your strategy and maximizing your impact. Let's dive into the nitty-gritty of how to analyze and optimize your Instagram performance.

First, let's talk about Instagram Insights, the built-in analytics tool available for business and creator accounts. Instagram Insights provides a wealth of data about your account's performance, including information about your audience, the reach and engagement of your posts, and the effectiveness of your Stories and ads. Accessing these insights is easy; just tap the menu icon in the top right corner of your profile and select Insights.

One of the most important sections of Instagram Insights is the Audience tab. Here, you can find detailed information about your followers, including their demographics, such as age, gender, and location. This data is crucial for understanding who your audience is and how to tailor your content to better meet their needs. For instance, if you discover that a significant portion of your followers are from a specific country, you might consider creating

CHAPTER 8: ANALYZING AND OPTIMIZING PERFORMANCE

content that caters to that region's culture and interests.

Another key metric to track is follower growth. This shows you how many followers you've gained or lost over a specific period. Sudden spikes or drops in follower count can indicate how your audience is responding to your content or other external factors. For example, if you see a significant increase in followers after running a giveaway, you'll know that this type of content resonates well with your audience.

Engagement metrics are another critical component of Instagram Insights. These include likes, comments, shares, and saves. High engagement rates indicate that your content is resonating with your audience and encouraging them to interact with it. Engagement rate is typically calculated by dividing the total number of engagements by the total number of followers and multiplying by 100 to get a percentage. Tracking engagement rates over time can help you identify trends and adjust your content strategy accordingly.

Reach and impressions are also important metrics to monitor. Reach refers to the number of unique users who have seen your post, while impressions indicate the total number of times your post has been viewed, including multiple views by the same user. A high reach means that your content is being seen by a large number of people, while a high number of impressions suggests that users are returning to view your content multiple times. Analyzing these metrics can help you understand how widely your content is being distributed and how engaging it is to your audience.

For Instagram Stories, metrics such as reach, impressions, taps forward, taps back, and exits provide valuable insights into how your audience is interacting with your Stories. Taps forward indicate that users are quickly moving through your content, which could mean that your Story isn't holding their attention. Taps back suggest that users are rewatching your content, which is generally a positive sign. Exits show where users are dropping off, helping you identify potential areas for improvement.

Now, let's talk about content optimization. Based on the insights you gather, you can make informed decisions to refine your content strategy. For instance, if you notice that posts with a certain type of content or at a specific time of day consistently perform better, you can adjust your strategy to create more of that content and post at those times. Similarly, if you see that your audience responds well to interactive Stories with polls and questions, you can incorporate more of these elements into your Stories.

Another important aspect of optimization is experimenting with different types of content and formats. Instagram offers a variety of content formats, including photos, videos, carousels, Stories, Reels, and IGTV. Experimenting with these different formats can help you identify which ones resonate best with your audience. For example, you might find that your followers engage more with videos than photos, or that Reels are particularly effective at attracting new followers.

Hashtags play a crucial role in optimizing your content for discovery. By analyzing the performance of your hashtags, you can determine which ones are driving the most reach and engagement. Tools like Instagram Insights and third-party analytics platforms can provide data on the performance of individual hashtags. Use this information to refine your hashtag strategy, focusing on the ones that yield the best results and experimenting with new ones to see if they can further boost your visibility.

Audience interaction is another key area to focus on for optimization. Engaging with your followers by responding to comments and messages can foster a sense of community and loyalty. Pay attention to the types of comments and questions your audience is leaving, as they can provide valuable insights into their preferences and interests. Use this feedback to tailor your content and engagement strategies to better meet their needs.

Collaborations and influencer partnerships can also benefit from performance analysis. Track the impact of these collaborations on your metrics, such as

CHAPTER 8: ANALYZING AND OPTIMIZING PERFORMANCE

follower growth, engagement rates, and reach. This data can help you assess the effectiveness of different partnerships and identify which influencers or brands are driving the most value for your account.

Ads performance is another critical area to analyze and optimize. If you're running Instagram ads, use the Ads Manager to track metrics such as reach, impressions, click-through rates, and conversions. Analyzing this data can help you understand which ad creatives and targeting strategies are most effective, allowing you to optimize your ad campaigns for better results.

Regularly reviewing and adjusting your content strategy based on performance data is essential for continuous improvement. Set aside time each week or month to analyze your metrics, identify trends, and make data-driven decisions. This iterative process will help you refine your strategy and ensure that your content remains relevant and engaging to your audience.

Benchmarking is another useful practice for performance analysis. Compare your metrics to industry benchmarks to see how you stack up against similar accounts. This can provide valuable context for your performance and help you set realistic goals for improvement. Industry benchmarks can vary based on factors such as account size, industry, and content type, so make sure you're comparing apples to apples.

Finally, stay informed about Instagram's algorithm updates and best practices. The platform is constantly evolving, and staying up-to-date with the latest changes can help you optimize your strategy and maintain a competitive edge. Follow Instagram's official blog and industry publications to keep abreast of new features, algorithm updates, and emerging trends.

Analyzing and optimizing your Instagram performance is an ongoing process that requires a combination of data analysis, strategic planning, and creative experimentation. By leveraging the insights provided by Instagram's analytics tools, experimenting with different content formats, and regularly reviewing your performance data, you can refine your strategy and maximize your impact on the platform. This approach will help you build a strong, engaged community and achieve your branding goals on Instagram.

Chapter 9: Monetizing Your Instagram Brand

Turning your Instagram presence into a money-making machine is the dream, isn't it? Whether you're a business looking to drive sales or an influencer wanting to cash in on your following, monetizing your Instagram brand is a goal within reach. The platform offers several avenues for revenue generation, from sponsored posts to selling products directly. Let's delve into the strategies for effectively monetizing your Instagram brand.

First, let's talk about sponsored posts and partnerships. Sponsored posts are when brands pay you to create content that promotes their products or services. These collaborations can be incredibly lucrative, especially if you have a large and engaged following. However, it's crucial to maintain authenticity. Your followers trust your recommendations, so only partner with brands that align with your values and will genuinely appeal to your audience.

When negotiating sponsorships, understand your worth. Brands are willing to pay for access to your audience, especially if you have high engagement rates. Consider creating a media kit that outlines your audience demographics, engagement metrics, and previous successful collaborations. This can help you present a professional image and justify your rates. Be transparent about sponsored content by using hashtags like #ad or #sponsored, not only to adhere to regulations but also to maintain trust with your followers.

Affiliate marketing is another effective way to monetize your Instagram brand. With affiliate marketing, you earn a commission for every sale made through a unique link you share. This can be a win-win situation if you partner with brands and products you genuinely love. To get started, join affiliate programs offered by companies or sign up with affiliate networks like Amazon Associates, ShareASale, or RewardStyle. Create content that highlights the benefits of the products, and always disclose your affiliate relationship to stay compliant with guidelines.

Instagram Shopping has revolutionized the way businesses can sell products directly on the platform. If you have a business account, you can set up an Instagram Shop and tag products in your posts, Stories, and Reels. This seamless integration allows followers to purchase items without ever leaving the app. To set up Instagram Shopping, connect your Instagram account to a Facebook catalog, either through Facebook's Business Manager, Shopify, or BigCommerce. Ensure your product images are high quality and your descriptions are clear and compelling to entice followers to buy.

Creating shoppable posts is a game-changer. When you tag products in your posts, make sure the images are visually appealing and the tags are strategically placed. Use captions to highlight the features and benefits of the products. Shoppable Stories are equally powerful. Use interactive stickers like product tags and links to drive traffic to your shop. This not only makes shopping convenient but also enhances the user experience.

Hosting giveaways and contests can boost engagement and attract new followers, but they can also be used strategically to drive sales. Partner with brands to offer a bundle of products as a prize and require participants to follow your account, like the post, and tag friends. This increases visibility and can lead to an uptick in followers and potential customers. Be clear about the rules and ensure the prizes are appealing to your target audience.

Another effective strategy for monetization is launching your own products or

CHAPTER 9: MONETIZING YOUR INSTAGRAM BRAND

merchandise. This works particularly well if you have a strong personal brand or a loyal community. Whether it's branded merchandise, digital products like e-books or courses, or a new line of physical products, having something unique to offer can drive significant revenue. Use your Instagram platform to tease new products, share behind-the-scenes content of the creation process, and build anticipation before the launch.

Crowdfunding is an emerging way to monetize your influence, especially for creatives and entrepreneurs. Platforms like Patreon allow your followers to support you financially in exchange for exclusive content, early access, or other perks. Promote your Patreon or other crowdfunding campaigns through your Instagram posts and Stories, highlighting the value and benefits supporters will receive. This can create a steady stream of income while fostering a closer connection with your most dedicated followers.

Live videos offer another revenue stream through Instagram's Live Badges feature. When you go live, followers can purchase badges to show their support. These badges appear as hearts next to the buyers' usernames during the live session. Engage with your audience in real-time, shout out badge buyers, and offer exclusive content or Q&A sessions to encourage more purchases. This direct form of monetization can be both profitable and engaging, deepening your connection with your audience.

Using Instagram's ads platform can drive traffic and sales to your website or products. Instagram ads allow you to target specific demographics, interests, and behaviors, making them highly effective for reaching potential customers. Experiment with different ad formats, such as photo ads, video ads, carousel ads, and Stories ads, to see which performs best for your goals. Monitor your ad performance using Instagram Insights and adjust your strategy based on the data to maximize your return on investment.

Collaborating with other influencers can also enhance monetization efforts. Joint campaigns, giveaways, and live sessions can help you tap into each other's audiences and increase your reach. When choosing collaborators, ensure their audience aligns with your target market and that their content style complements yours. Successful collaborations can result in increased followers, higher engagement, and more sales.

Hosting virtual events, workshops, or webinars can be an effective way to monetize your expertise. Charge a fee for attendees to join and provide valuable content, such as tutorials, industry insights, or exclusive Q&A sessions. Promote these events through your Instagram posts, Stories, and ads to attract attendees. Virtual events not only generate revenue but also position you as an authority in your niche.

Brand ambassadorships are another lucrative opportunity. Unlike one-off sponsored posts, brand ambassadorships involve a longer-term relationship where you regularly promote a brand's products or services. This can provide a steady income stream and deeper integration of the brand into your content. When negotiating ambassadorships, ensure the terms align with your brand values and that you have creative control to maintain authenticity.

Leveraging analytics is crucial for effective monetization. Regularly review your Instagram Insights to understand which types of content drive the most engagement and conversions. Pay attention to metrics like reach, impressions, engagement rates, and website clicks. Use this data to refine your strategy, focusing on content that resonates most with your audience and drives sales. Adjust your posting schedule, content format, and promotional tactics based on the insights to maximize your revenue potential.

Building an email list from your Instagram followers can also enhance monetization. Use lead magnets like free downloads, exclusive content, or discounts to encourage followers to subscribe to your email list. With an email list, you can directly market to your audience, driving traffic and sales outside of Instagram. Promote your email list through posts and Stories, and provide valuable content to keep subscribers engaged and more likely to convert into

CHAPTER 9: MONETIZING YOUR INSTAGRAM BRAND

customers.

Finally, stay informed about new features and trends on Instagram. The platform continually evolves, introducing new tools and opportunities for monetization. Whether it's a new shopping feature, an algorithm change, or a trending content format, staying ahead of the curve can give you a competitive edge. Follow industry news, join relevant communities, and experiment with new features to find innovative ways to monetize your Instagram brand.

Monetizing your Instagram brand requires a strategic approach, combining sponsored posts, affiliate marketing, Instagram Shopping, and various other methods. By understanding your audience, leveraging analytics, and staying adaptable, you can turn your Instagram presence into a profitable venture. With consistent effort and creativity, the potential for monetizing your brand on Instagram is limitless.

Chapter 10: Staying Ahead of the Curve

Instagram is a dynamic platform that evolves at a pace that can sometimes feel overwhelming. What worked yesterday might not work tomorrow, and staying ahead of the curve is crucial for maintaining a competitive edge. Keeping up with updates, experimenting with new trends, and continuously learning are key components of staying relevant and successful on Instagram. Let's delve into strategies for ensuring your Instagram presence remains fresh, innovative, and effective.

First, let's talk about staying informed. Instagram frequently rolls out new features, algorithm changes, and policy updates. Being aware of these changes as soon as they happen can give you a significant advantage. Follow Instagram's official blog and social media channels to get the latest updates directly from the source. Industry websites and social media marketing blogs are also excellent resources for staying informed about new features and best practices.

Participating in webinars and online courses can provide in-depth knowledge and insights into the latest Instagram trends and strategies. Many social media experts and marketing platforms offer free or affordable webinars that cover a range of topics, from advanced analytics to creative content ideas. These resources can help you stay up-to-date with the latest techniques and tools for maximizing your Instagram presence.

CHAPTER 10: STAYING AHEAD OF THE CURVE

Engaging with the Instagram community can also keep you ahead of the curve. Join groups, forums, and communities where social media marketers and influencers share their experiences and insights. Platforms like Reddit, Facebook Groups, and LinkedIn offer spaces for professionals to discuss the latest trends, share tips, and provide feedback. Being an active member of these communities can provide valuable insights and inspiration for your own strategy.

Experimentation is crucial for staying ahead on Instagram. The platform's constant evolution means there's always something new to try, whether it's a new content format, a creative tool, or a trending topic. Don't be afraid to test new ideas and formats. Monitor the results and use the data to refine your strategy. Successful experimentation can lead to innovative content that sets your brand apart from the competition.

Leveraging data and analytics is essential for informed decision-making. Regularly review your Instagram Insights to track the performance of your content and understand your audience's preferences. Pay attention to metrics like reach, impressions, engagement rates, and follower growth. Analyzing this data can help you identify trends and adjust your strategy accordingly. For example, if you notice that a particular type of content consistently performs well, you can create more of that content to maintain high engagement levels.

Adapting to algorithm changes is another important aspect of staying ahead. Instagram's algorithm determines which content is shown to users based on factors like engagement, relevancy, and timeliness. Understanding how the algorithm works and adjusting your strategy to align with its criteria can help ensure your content reaches the maximum number of users. Keep an eye on industry news and updates to stay informed about any algorithm changes and how they might impact your strategy.

Trends play a significant role in keeping your content fresh and engaging. Identifying and participating in relevant trends can boost your visibility and engagement. Use tools like Google Trends, Instagram's Explore page, and social media listening tools to stay on top of emerging trends. When you spot a trend that aligns with your brand, put your own unique spin on it to make it relevant and engaging for your audience.

Seasonal and event-based content can also keep your Instagram presence dynamic. Plan your content calendar around major holidays, cultural events, and industry-specific occasions. Creating timely and relevant content for these events can increase your visibility and engagement. Use relevant hashtags and participate in event-related conversations to expand your reach.

Collaborations and partnerships can provide fresh content and new perspectives for your Instagram feed. Partnering with influencers, brands, or industry experts can introduce your brand to new audiences and create exciting content that resonates with both your followers and theirs. Choose collaborators whose values and aesthetics align with your brand to ensure a cohesive and authentic partnership.

Continuous learning is essential for staying ahead of the curve. The social media landscape is constantly changing, and staying informed about the latest trends, tools, and best practices can help you maintain a competitive edge. Attend industry conferences, read books by social media experts, and take online courses to expand your knowledge and skills. Staying curious and open to new ideas will keep your Instagram strategy innovative and effective.

Innovation often comes from looking beyond your own industry. Draw inspiration from brands and influencers in different niches to find new ideas and perspectives. Analyze their content, engagement strategies, and overall approach to see what you can adapt and apply to your own strategy. This cross-industry inspiration can lead to creative and unique content that stands out.

Maintaining flexibility in your strategy is also important. While it's crucial to have a well-defined plan, being able to pivot and adapt to new trends and changes is equally important. Regularly review your strategy and be willing to make adjustments based on performance data, industry trends, and feedback from your audience. This flexibility will allow you to stay relevant and continue growing your Instagram presence.

Personalization is becoming increasingly important in social media marketing. Tailoring your content to your audience's preferences and behaviors can significantly boost engagement and loyalty. Use data and insights to understand your audience's interests, needs, and pain points. Create content that speaks directly to them, addressing their concerns and providing value. Personalized content makes your audience feel seen and appreciated, fostering a deeper connection with your brand.

Interactive content can enhance engagement and keep your audience interested. Use features like polls, questions, quizzes, and live videos to encourage interaction. Interactive content not only boosts engagement but also provides valuable feedback and insights into your audience's preferences. This can inform your content strategy and help you create more relevant and engaging posts.

Visual storytelling is a powerful tool for capturing your audience's attention and conveying your brand's message. Use high-quality images, videos, and graphics to tell compelling stories that resonate with your followers. Consistent visual branding, including colors, fonts, and overall aesthetic, helps create a cohesive and recognizable brand identity. Visual storytelling not only makes your content more engaging but also helps build an emotional connection with your audience.

User-generated content (UGC) continues to be a valuable asset for brands. Encouraging your followers to create and share content related to your brand can provide authentic, high-quality content and foster a sense of community. Reposting UGC shows appreciation for your followers' contributions and can inspire others to share their own experiences. Use branded hashtags and run UGC campaigns to encourage participation and highlight the best content.

Social listening is a crucial practice for staying ahead of the curve. Monitor conversations and trends related to your brand, industry, and competitors. Social listening tools can help you track mentions, hashtags, and keywords, providing valuable insights into what your audience is talking about and what's trending. Use this information to inform your content strategy, address customer concerns, and identify opportunities for engagement.

Engaging with your audience is key to building a loyal community and staying relevant. Respond to comments, direct messages, and mentions promptly and authentically. Show appreciation for your followers' support and contributions. Engaging with your audience not only boosts loyalty but also provides valuable feedback and insights into their needs and preferences.

Regularly reviewing and refining your Instagram strategy is essential for continuous improvement. Set aside time each month to analyze your performance data, review your content calendar, and assess your overall strategy. Identify what's working well and what needs improvement. Use this information to make data-driven decisions and adjust your strategy as needed. Continuous refinement ensures that your Instagram presence remains effective and aligned with your goals.

Staying ahead of the curve on Instagram requires a combination of staying informed, experimenting with new ideas, leveraging data, and maintaining flexibility. By following these strategies, you can keep your content fresh, engaging, and relevant, ensuring long-term success on the platform. Embrace the dynamic nature of Instagram and stay proactive in adapting to changes and trends. This approach will help you build a strong, resilient, and innovative Instagram presence that continues to thrive.

Conclusion: Wrapping It All Up

As we reach the end of this journey through Instagram branding, it's time to bring together all the threads we've woven. Instagram is a complex and dynamic platform, but with the right strategies and a bit of creativity, you can master it and build a strong, engaging brand presence. Let's recap and delve deeper into the core principles and strategies that can drive your success on Instagram.

Understanding Instagram as a platform is the foundation. Instagram's evolution from a simple photo-sharing app to a powerful marketing tool underscores its importance in today's digital landscape. With over a billion active users monthly, it offers a vast audience for brands to tap into. The key is to understand the demographics and behaviors of Instagram users, which predominantly include younger audiences but also span across various age groups. This insight helps in tailoring your content to resonate with your target audience effectively.

Setting up your profile for success is your first step in this journey. Your profile is your digital storefront and needs to make a strong impression. A compelling bio that clearly conveys who you are and what you offer, a recognizable profile picture, and a cohesive aesthetic are essential. Consistency in visual elements helps in building a recognizable brand identity. Highlights can showcase important content and ensure new visitors understand what your brand is about quickly.

Developing your brand aesthetic is where your creativity shines. A cohesive visual identity makes your brand memorable and helps it stand out. Choosing a consistent color palette, using specific filters, and maintaining a particular photography style are all part of creating a visual brand language. This visual consistency should extend across all your content formats, from regular posts to Stories and Reels. It's not just about looking good; it's about conveying your brand's personality and values visually.

Content creation is the heartbeat of your Instagram strategy. High-quality content that engages and resonates with your audience is crucial. This includes a variety of content types like photos, videos, carousels, Stories, Reels, and IGTV. Each format serves a unique purpose and can be used to keep your feed dynamic and interesting. Planning your content through a calendar ensures consistency and helps in strategically aligning your posts with key dates and events.

Building a community is about more than just gaining followers; it's about fostering engagement and loyalty. Engaging with your audience through comments, direct messages, and interactive content like polls and questions can build a loyal community. User-generated content is a powerful tool for engagement, as it makes followers feel valued and involved. Contests, giveaways, and collaborations can further enhance community building by making your followers feel like an integral part of your brand.

Leveraging hashtags and trends is a smart way to increase visibility and engagement. Hashtags categorize your content and make it discoverable to a broader audience. Using a mix of popular, niche, and branded hashtags can help you reach different segments of your audience. Staying on top of trends and participating in them strategically can give your content a visibility boost. It's about being relevant and tapping into what's currently engaging users.

Using Instagram Stories effectively can significantly enhance your engagement. Stories offer a more casual and immediate way to connect with your audience. Utilizing features like stickers, polls, questions, and countdowns can make your Stories interactive and engaging. Highlights allow you to extend the life of your Stories and keep important content accessible. Regularly posting Stories and using them to share behind-the-scenes content, user-generated content, and educational tips can keep your audience engaged.

Analyzing and optimizing performance is where you turn data into action. Instagram Insights provide valuable data on your audience, content performance, and engagement. Regularly reviewing these metrics can help you understand what works and what doesn't. Metrics like reach, impressions, engagement rates, and follower growth are crucial for tracking your progress. Using this data to refine your strategy ensures that you are continually improving and adapting to your audience's preferences.

Monetizing your Instagram brand opens up various revenue streams. Sponsored posts, affiliate marketing, Instagram Shopping, and selling your own products or services are some of the ways to monetize. Each method requires a strategic approach, whether it's negotiating sponsorship deals, creating engaging affiliate content, or setting up an Instagram Shop. Understanding your audience and providing value through your content is key to successful monetization.

Staying ahead of the curve involves continuous learning and adaptation. Instagram is constantly evolving, and staying informed about new features, trends, and best practices is essential. Engaging with the Instagram community, participating in webinars, and following industry news can keep you updated. Experimentation and flexibility in your strategy allow you to adapt to changes and keep your content fresh and relevant.

The journey of building a strong Instagram brand is ongoing. It requires a combination of strategic planning, creative content, engagement with your audience, and continuous optimization. By understanding the platform, setting up a compelling profile, developing a cohesive brand aesthetic, creating engaging content, building a community, leveraging hashtags and trends, using Stories effectively, analyzing performance, monetizing strategically, and staying ahead of the curve, you can create a powerful and impactful Instagram presence.

Instagram is more than just a social media platform; it's a space where brands can connect with their audience on a personal level, tell their story, and grow their business. Embrace the tools, strategies, and insights shared in this guide, and you'll be well on your way to Instagram success. Remember, the key to thriving on Instagram is not just about following trends but about creating genuine connections and delivering value to your audience. Keep experimenting, stay adaptable, and enjoy the creative journey.

Made in the USA
Las Vegas, NV
13 July 2024